Animal Tr[icks]

T0337162

Glow in
the Dark

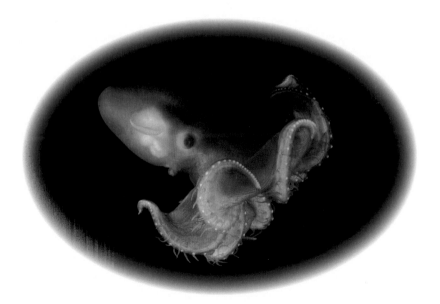

Written by Rob Alcraft

Collins

Make light

Some creatures can make their own light.
This can be very useful!

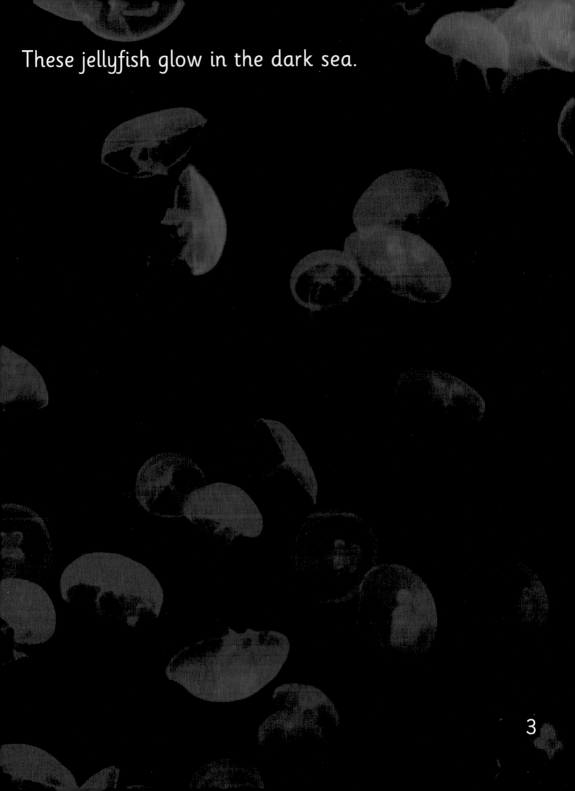

These jellyfish glow in the dark sea.

3

Glow and sparkle

Creatures that can glow in the dark have chemicals inside their bodies.

These magical lights are glow worms.

When these chemicals mix, they make light.

glowing sucker octopus

Be seen

When it's dark, a little sparkle can help some creatures find a mate.

These twinkling, sparkly lights are fireflies.

A firefly displays its glowing tail.

Be crafty

Some creatures use light to catch food.

An angler fish dangles a bobble of light to tempt little creatures to come close.

Its large mouth then gobbles them up!

Be invisible

Creatures can use light to make themselves hard to spot.

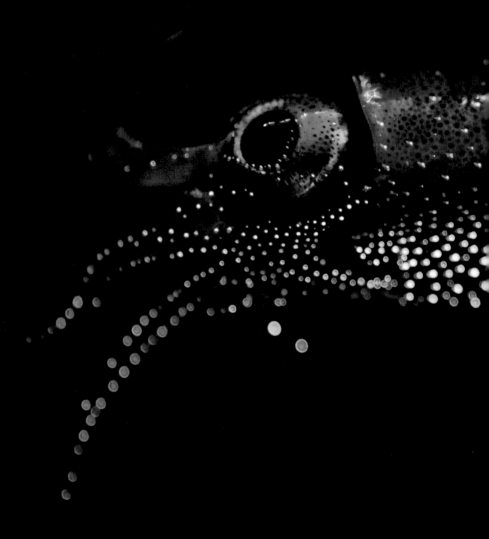

Firefly squid cover themselves in tiny dots of light to blur their outlines and confuse predators.

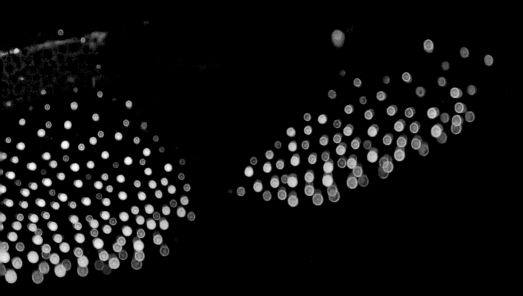

Be scary

Some creatures use light to startle hungry predators – while they dodge away.

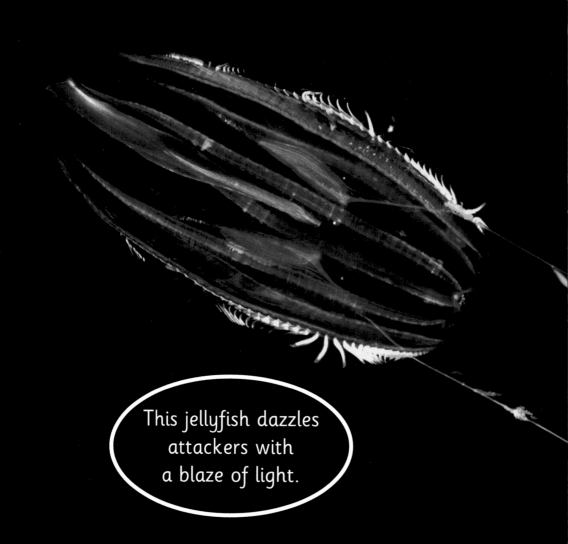

This jellyfish dazzles attackers with a blaze of light.

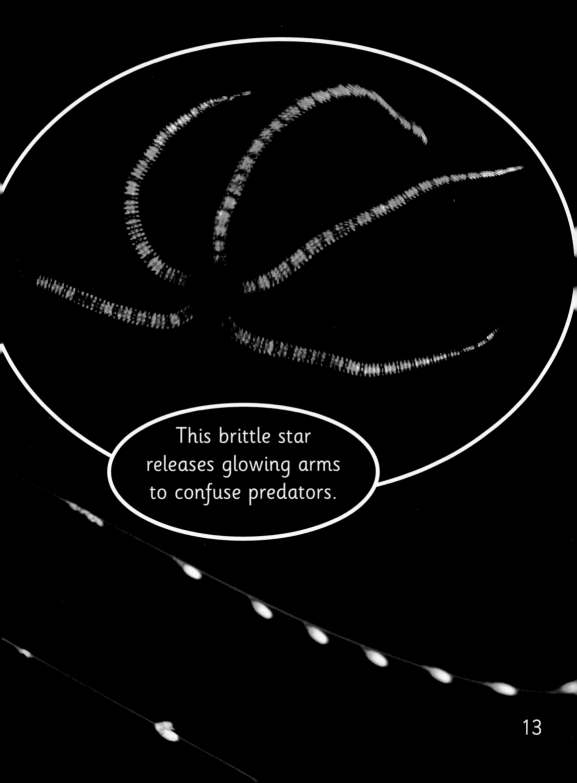

This brittle star releases glowing arms to confuse predators.

Be bright

Even very tiny creatures like plankton can use light to protect themselves.

Sea sparkle is a giant cloud of plankton. When it glows, predators swim away.

Be safe

Some creatures use light to show predators that they have a horrible flavour!

click beetle   railroad worm

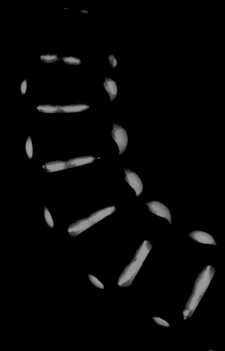

Their glowing colours tell predators they are not good to eat.

glowing millipede

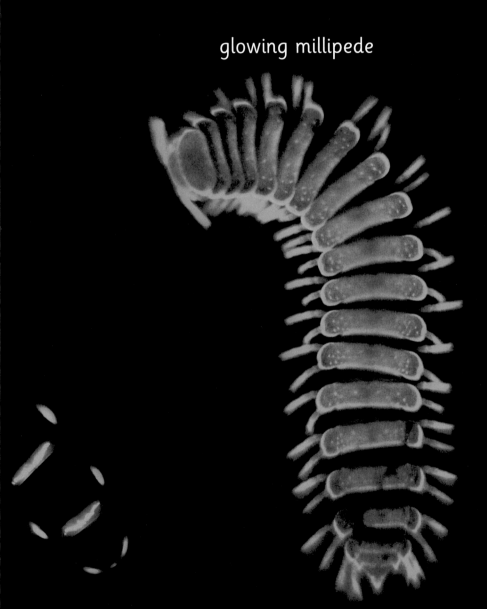

Be chatty

Some creatures communicate with light.

This sea pickle is a giant group of tiny creatures.

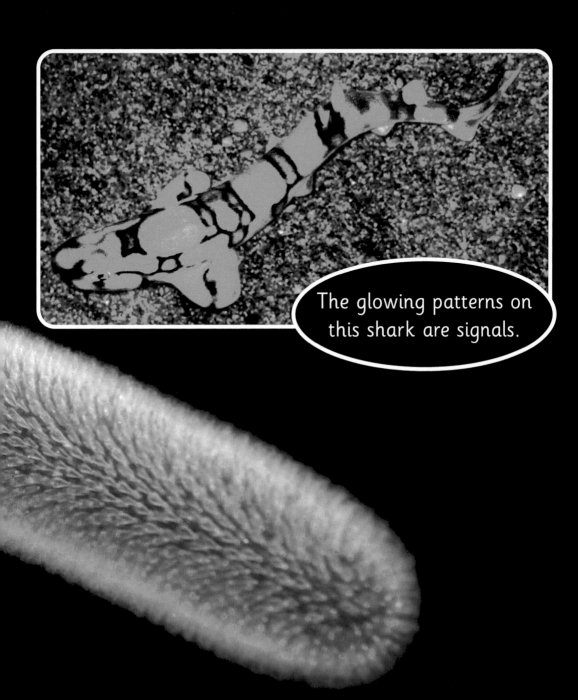

The glowing patterns on this shark are signals.

Be sparkly

See how useful it can be to glow?
When it's inky dark, a little
sparkle can help catch food,
dodge predators or find a mate.

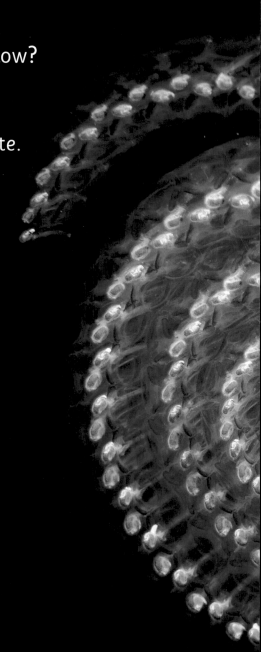

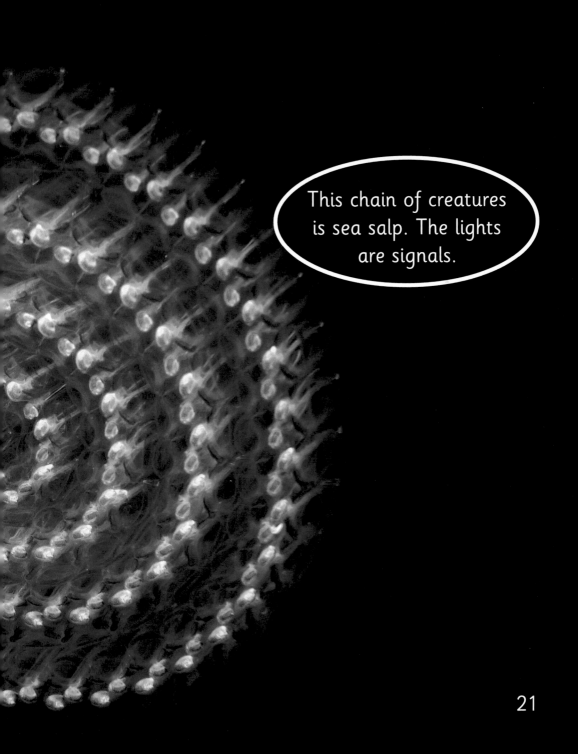

This chain of creatures is sea salp. The lights are signals.

Why do some creatures glow?

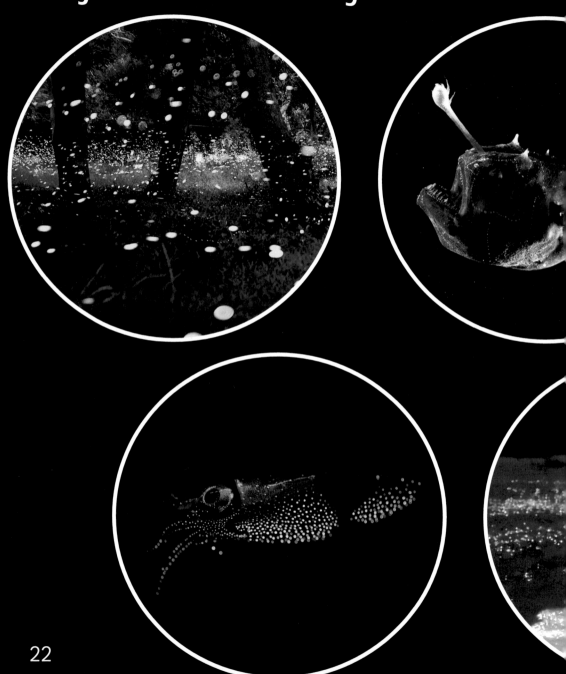

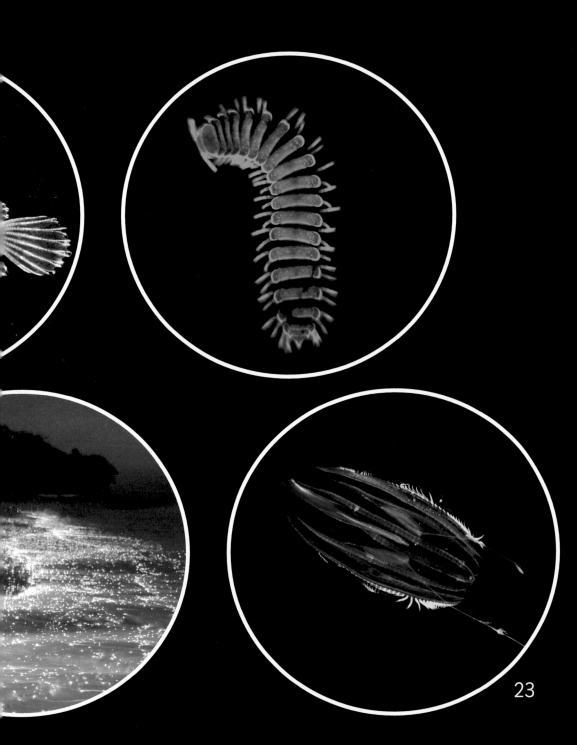

After reading

Letters and Sounds: Phase 5

Word count: 298

Focus phonemes: /ch/ tch, t /j/ g, ge, dge /l/ le /w/ wh /v/ ve /c/ ch /ai/ a /ee/ e, y, e-e /oo/ u /igh/ ie, y

Common exception words: of, to, the, are, their

Curriculum links: Science: Animals including humans

National Curriculum learning objectives: Reading/word reading: apply phonic knowledge and skills as the route to decode words, read other words of more than one syllable that contain taught GPCs; Reading/comprehension: drawing on what they already know or on background information and vocabulary provided by the teacher

Developing fluency

- Your child may enjoy hearing you read the book.
- Read the first double page then take turns to read a section. Challenge your child to read as if they are reading to younger children. How interesting can they make the creatures sound?

Phonic practice

- Remind your child to break down longer words into chunks as they read these words.

  use/ful   con/fuse

  pred/at/ors   comm/un/ic/ate

Extending vocabulary

- Ask your child to think of a synonym (word with a similar meaning) for each of the following:

  sparkle (e.g. *twinkle, glitter*)   confuse (e.g. *muddle, baffle*)

  glow (e.g. *gleam, shine*)   startle (e.g. *surprise, shock*)

  crafty (e.g. *clever, sneaky*)   dazzles (e.g. *dazes, blinds*)